The OLYMPIANS

Rob Waring, *Series Editor*

NATIONAL
GEOGRAPHIC
L E A R N I N G

Australia · Brazil · Mexico · Singapore · United Kingdom · United States

Words to Know

This story is set in the country of Greece, which is part of Europe. It's about the Olympic Games, which started long ago in a place called Olympia.

 Olympic Events. Read the definitions and look at the picture. Write the number of the correct <u>underlined</u> word or phrase next to each Olympic event participant.

1. A <u>discus thrower</u> throws a heavy plate-shaped object as far as possible.
2. <u>Boxers</u> are fighters who hit other fighters with their hands to earn points.
3. <u>Wrestlers</u> fight by holding other fighters and trying to throw them down.
4. A <u>javelin thrower</u> throws a long stick with a pointed end.
5. A <u>long jumper</u> runs and then jumps as far forward as possible.

Ancient Olympians Practicing for Events

B **Olympic Winners.** Read the paragraph. Then match each word with the correct definition.

Olympic champions are very skilled people who have won an Olympic event. They have shown that they are stronger, faster, or more skilled than their opponents. In ancient Greece, Olympic event winners received an olive wreath to wear on their head. They were treated almost as if they were part gods, or demigods. In modern times, winning athletes are given a different prize. Each Olympic winner gets a medal that is made of gold at a special ceremony.

1. champion _____

2. opponent _____

3. olive wreath _____

4. demigod _____

5. athlete _____

6. medal _____

a. a being who is part man and part god

b. the person who has beaten all other competitors

c. a small, metal circle given to the winner of a competition

d. a person who is very good at sports and who often competes in organized events

e. a person who takes the opposite side in a fight, game, etc.

f. a circle of olive leaves which was a sign of distinction long ago

olive wreath

gold medal

Olympic Winners Then and Now

Today, the Olympic Games, or the 'Olympics,' happen every four years and are held in a different country each time. At the Olympics, top athletes from around the world come together to test their skills and determination in individual or team sports. It's an opportunity for them to compete against the world's other great sportsmen and women for Olympic medals. Olympic gold medals, which are given only to the winner or winners of each competition, are the lifetime dream of athletes everywhere. However, in order to understand the modern Olympics better, we must return to the origin of the Olympic Games: Greece.

 CD 2, Track 03

Skim for Gist

Read through the entire book quickly to answer the questions.

1. Which is the basic focus of the story: the past or present Olympic Games?

2. What is Olympia and why is it important to the story?

Olympia, Greece was the home of the ancient Olympic games.

For the ancient Greeks, the Olympic Games represented the highest form of physical achievement. The games were a mix of athletic skill and religion. They were celebrated in a festival which was **dedicated to**[1] the Greek god Zeus. The ancient Greeks believed that Zeus was the king of the gods, and therefore he was considered to be the most powerful of them all.

The Olympics were also a time of political calm. During the period when the Olympic Games were happening, there was peace across all the land. Athletes traveled from all over the ancient Greek world to compete in events in beautiful, green Olympia. At the time, Olympia was a special place of peace that was used only for Olympic events and religious or political meetings.

---

[1]**dedicated to:** when an event is dedicated to someone or something, it is held to show respect for that person or thing

The Greek God Zeus

According to legend, a runner named **Coroebus**[2] was the first Olympic champion in 776 B.C. He was a local cook who was fast enough to defeat all the other competitors in a foot race. Foot races, like the one which Coroebus won, were central events in the ancient games at the time. Only men could compete in the races and they wore no shoes or clothes. They were covered only in **olive oil**[3] as they ran down a straight path. These races took place in front of huge crowds of as many as 40,000 people.

---

[2] **Coroebus:** [kərɔɪbəs]
[3] **olive oil:** an oil used for cooking that comes from a small black or green fruit called an olive

Over the centuries, the Olympic Games developed and changed, and the competitions became more serious. Olympic rules were created which required Olympians to train for at least ten months before the big event. These same rules also required participants to maintain a demanding training plan just before the games. They had to train with expert judges for the 30 days before they competed.

Being able to run fast continued to be a very important skill, but the games quickly got bigger and began to include more than just running. They also started to include the **pentathlon**[4] events. The pentathlon included five sports: discus throwing, javelin throwing, running, long jumping, and wrestling. Several of these activities are still recognizable today as parts of the modern-day **decathlon**[5] or as individual events.

---

[4] **pentathlon:** an Olympic event in which athletes participate in five different sports NOTE: today's pentathlon sports differ from the ancient event's sports
[5] **decathlon:** a modern-day Olympic event in which athletes participate in ten challenging sports over two days

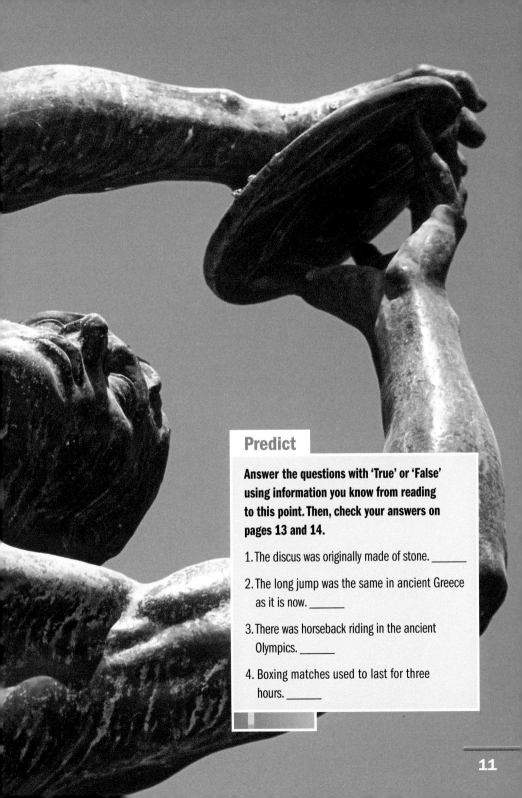

Predict

Answer the questions with 'True' or 'False'
using information you know from reading
to this point. Then, check your answers on
pages 13 and 14.

1. The discus was originally made of stone. _____

2. The long jump was the same in ancient Greece
   as it is now. _____

3. There was horseback riding in the ancient
   Olympics. _____

4. Boxing matches used to last for three
   hours. _____

Many of the individual sports that were included in the ancient pentathlon were basically the same as they are now. Others were performed differently or used different equipment. Discus throwers, for example, competed in much the same way that they do now, but their discus was made of stone. Later, this stone discus was replaced by ones that were made with various metals, such as **bronze**.[6]

The long jump was slightly different in the ancient Olympics. Long jumpers used to run quickly down a track, or path, towards the jump area just as they do today. However, at that time, the jumpers held weights in their hands to give them more **momentum**.[7] This extra weight helped to push the athletes through the air when they jumped.

The javelin-throwing event has remained basically the same. The sport probably came directly from the skills that people used when they hunted animals. The javelins that were used in the ancient Olympic Games were very much like those of the modern games. They were pointed wooden sticks that were about the same height as a man. However, the javelins that were used in the ancient Olympics had a special leather finger holder on them. This gave the throwers more power and **accuracy**[8] so they were able to throw greater distances.

---

[6]**bronze:** a brown metal made of copper (Cu) and tin (Sn)
[7]**momentum:** the force that keeps an object moving
[8]**accuracy:** the ability to hit a target

While some ancient Olympic events required determination and strength, others focused on one thing: speed. **Equestrian**[9] events, which happened in the riding ring of the Hippodrome, consisted of chariot racing and horseback riding. In chariot racing, a two-wheeled vehicle was driven by a man and pulled by horses. In horseback riding, men rode on the backs of horses and used only their legs to hold on. Both of these events focused purely on being the fastest person in the race.

The Palaestra was the ancient Greek wrestling and boxing training area. In wrestling, the winner was the first man to throw his opponent to the ground three times. Boxing matches in the ancient games had no time limits. Boxers wrapped pieces of leather around their **wrists**[10] for support and fought as long as they could. This was usually until one man said that he was defeated or one was hit so hard that he could no longer fight. Surprisingly, in wrestling and boxing size and weight were not important. Competitors were placed in just two categories: one for men and the other for boys.

---

[9]**equestrian:** [ɪkwɛstriən] connected with the riding of horses
[10]**wrist:** the part of the body that connects the hand and the arm

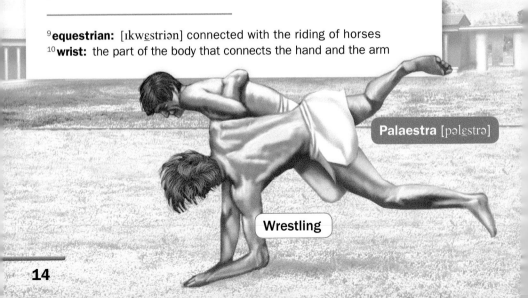

Palaestra [pəlɛstrə]

Wrestling

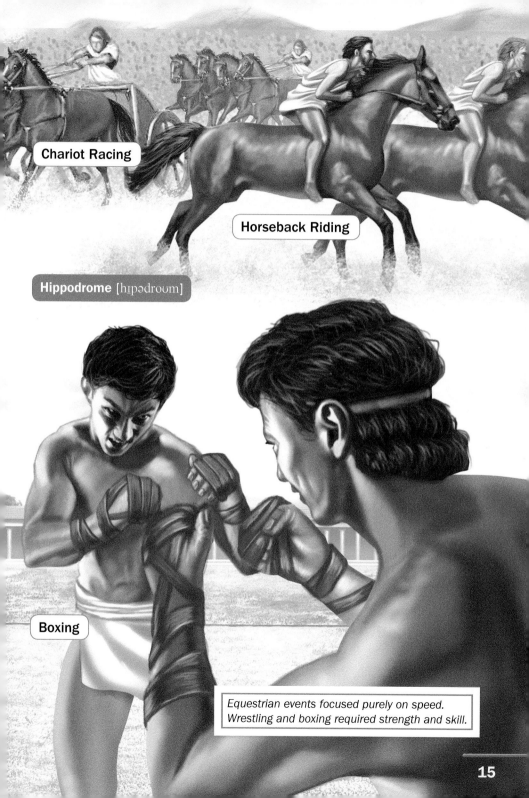

Chariot Racing

Horseback Riding

Hippodrome [hɪpədroʊm]

Boxing

Equestrian events focused purely on speed. Wrestling and boxing required strength and skill.

Winning an event in the ancient Olympics was quite different from winning one in today's games. Nowadays, athletes receive gold, silver, and bronze medals for finishing an event in first, second, or third place. In ancient times, though, there was only one winner for each event. The prize for winning was not a medal, but an olive wreath. At the time, an Olympic olive wreath was a sign of distinction, or social position, for an athlete. Winners of this valuable prize could return to their village as highly respected individuals. Many people in ancient Greece regarded Olympic champions as demigods, so they were thought to be especially great.

Unfortunately, the Olympic Games weren't considered to be a special event by everyone. In 393 A.D., nearly 12 centuries after they first started, the Olympic Games were stopped by Roman **Emperor Theodosius I**.[11] He decided that there would be no more festivals that were related to ancient religious figures.

---

[11] **Emperor Theodosius I:** Theodosius [θiədouʃəs] the First was a ruler in ancient Greece

It was another 1,500 years before the Olympic Games were brought back to life in modern times. The first modern international Olympic Games were held in Athens in 1896. Since then, the Olympics have developed into one of the world's most important sporting events.

The ancient Greek Olympic Games have survived the test of time and history. Although they have changed over the years, one thing has always remained the same: the games still celebrate sports in the exciting Olympian way!

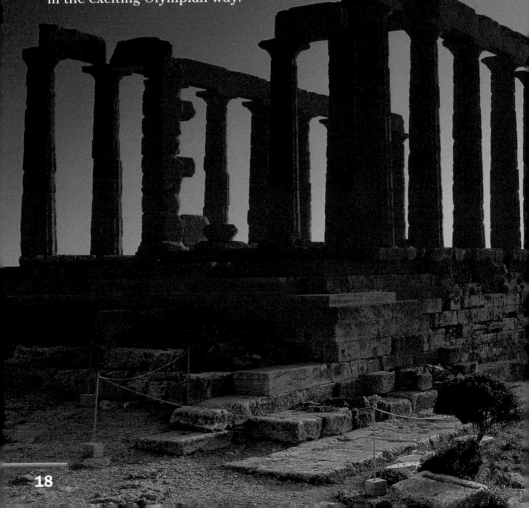

After You Read

1. On page 4, the word 'determination' means:
   A. manners
   B. will to succeed
   C. speed
   D. religion

2. Why does the writer talk about the origin of the Olympics?
   A. to teach about the history of the games
   B. to introduce Olympus
   C. to show how the medals were designed
   D. to show that winning the Olympics is a dream

3. Why were the ancient games dedicated to the Greek god Zeus?
   A. He was the god of games.
   B. He was the strongest god.
   C. He was the god of athletes.
   D. He was the fastest god.

4. Which of the following is NOT true about the ancient foot races?
   A. The runners were covered in olive oil.
   B. It was the most important event.
   C. Men ran without shoes.
   D. The competitors ran without an audience.

5. The writer probably thinks that competing in the ancient Olympics was:
   A. never serious
   B. optional
   C. difficult
   D. painful

6. In paragraph 2 on page 10, 'they' refers to the:
   A. runners
   B. rules
   C. judges
   D. games

7. How are the ancient pentathlon and the modern decathlon different?
   A. They are not different.
   B. The pentathlon had more events.
   C. The decathlon has more events.
   D. There was no ancient pentathlon.

8. In paragraph 1 on page 14, the word 'required' can be replaced by:
   A. prepared
   B. needed
   C. defeated
   D. permitted

9. What does the writer think was unusual about wrestling and boxing?
   A. Athletes hit the ground.
   B. Men wore leather wristbands.
   C. Each match was timed.
   D. There were only two categories: men and boys.

10. Why was the olive wreath valuable as a prize?
    A. It gave the winner a high social position.
    B. It was more expensive than gold.
    C. The village people wanted to sell it.
    D. It turned the athletes into gods.

11. How did Theodosius I feel about the games?
    A. He wanted them to be religious.
    B. He enjoyed watching them.
    C. He was opposed to them.
    D. He wanted athletes to win medals.

12. What's a good heading for page 18?
    A. Games Return after Three Centuries
    B. Olympic Feeling Remains Unchanged
    C. Athens Hosts Every Olympics
    D. Modern Festival Lacks History

Amazing Olympic
CHAMPIONS

Michael Johnson

During the 1996 Olympic Games in the U.S. city of Atlanta, Michael Johnson competed in both the 200-meter* and 400-meter events. No one had ever done this before. He wore a special pair of gold shoes and people started calling him "The Man with the Golden Shoes." Johnson ran the 400-meter race in 43.49 seconds—almost a second faster than his opponent, Roger Black of Great Britain. He then went on to win the 200-meter race with 19.32 seconds. At one point, he was running at almost 25 miles per hour! Johnson went on to win five gold medals in his career and holds three world records as of 2007.

Heike Gabriela Drechsler

German Heike Drechsler is one of the most successful female long jumpers of all time. She is the only woman who has won two Olympic gold medals in the long jump. On August 7, 1992, at the Olympic Games in Barcelona, Spain, Drechsler won a gold medal with a winning jump of 7.14 meters. In the same year, she recorded the year's longest jump of 7.48 meters,

Heike Gabriela Drechsler

*See page 24 for a metric conversion chart

Olympic Champions

Sport	Athlete	Home Country	Personal Best	Where/When
400-Meter Race	Michael Johnson	USA	43.18 seconds	Seville, Spain /1999
Long Jump	Heike Drechsler	Germany	7.48 meters	Laussane, Switzerland /1992
Javelin	Jan Železný	Czech Republic	98.48 meters	Jena, Germany /1996

which became her career best. In 2000, in Sydney, Australia, she won another gold with a jump of 7.23 meters. As of 2000, Drechsler had won more than 400 long jump competitions with results over seven meters. This is more than any other female athlete in history.

Jan Železný

Many people think that Jan Železný is the greatest javelin thrower ever. He won a silver medal in the 1988 Olympics as well as gold medals at the 1992, 1996, and 2000 Olympic Games. In addition, he won three World Championship titles in 1993, 1995, and 2001. He set the world record in 1996 when he threw the javelin a distance of 98.48 meters. In his career, Železný has made 52 throws of over 90 meters—more than all other javelin throwers together. Some people think his success is partly due to his family background. Both of his parents were javelin throwers, and his first coach was his father.

CD 2, Track 04

Word Count: 346
Time: _____

Vocabulary List

accuracy (13)
athlete (3, 4, 7, 13, 17)
boxer (2, 14)
bronze (13, 17)
champion (3, 8, 17)
decathlon (10)
dedicated to (7)
demigod (3, 17)
discus thrower (2, 10, 13)
equestrian (14, 15)
javelin thrower (2, 10, 13)
long jumper (2, 10, 13)
medal (3, 4, 17)
momentum (13)
olive oil (8)
olive wreath (3, 17)
opponent (3, 14)
pentathlon (10, 13)
wrestler (2, 14)
wrist (14)

Metric Conversion Chart

Area
1 hectare = 2.471 acres

Length
1 centimeter = .394 inches
1 meter = 1.094 yards
1 kilometer = .621 miles

Temperature
0° Celsius = 32° Fahrenheit

Volume
1 liter = 1.057 quarts

Weight
1 gram = .035 ounces
1 kilogram = 2.2 pounds